Poems for Medical Students

Poems for Medical Students

An Anthology

Edited by

Dr Roger Bloor
Dr Karen Schofield
Dr Bruce Summers

University of Keele
Medical School
Medical Humanities

First Printing, 2019
Second Edition, 2020
Third Edition 2021

Published for Keele University
by Clayhanger Press

ISBN-13: 978-1-9162001-0-4

Acknowledgments

The publication of this anthology was made possible through the generous financial support of -

Dr Lisetta Lovett
Dr Jonathan Lovett
Professor Christian Mallen
Professor Fidelma O'Mahony
Professor Peter Coventry
Dr Srinivasan Koottalai
Dr Meena Srinivasan
Mr Bruce Summers
The School of Humanities , Keele University

The editors are grateful for the advice and guidance provided by – Teresa Heath

Profits from the sale of this book are used to fund the distribution of a free copy to all new Medical Students at Keele University

Table of Contents

Acknowledgments iii

Introduction 6

About Being a Doctor

Advice to a Medical Student - Michael Swann 12

Venipuncture - John Graham-Pole 14

Junior Doctor Learning Log - Karen Schofield 15

The Apprentice Surgeon - Michael Salcman 16

Today I do not want to be a doctor - Glenn Colquhoun 18

Today I want to be a doctor - Glenn Colquhoun 19

In All Those Years At Medical School - Roger Bloor 20

it's about a man - Wendy French 21

How to Behave with the Ill - Julia Darling 22

About Disease

Four Years After Diagnosis - Angela Narciso Torres 27

A Seagull Murmur - Robin Robertson 28

Migraine - Fiona Sampson 29

Myeloma Moths - Karen Schofield 30

Mammogram - Jo McDougall 31

Coma - Mimi Khalvati 32

The Memory Clinic - Roger Bloor 33

Chemo Nurse - Keith Chandler 34

About Being A Patient

In Intensive Care - Olivia Byard   39

Too Heavy - Julia Darling   40

Plane tree outside Ward 78 - Helen Dunmore   42

Leaving the Hospital - Anya Silver   43

Notes

The Poets   45

Notes on the Poets   46

Sources of Illustrations   50

Permissions   51

Introduction

Congratulations on becoming a medical student.

Your undergraduate course is just the first stage of a process of medical education which will go on for as long as you practice as a doctor. Becoming a doctor is a challenging but exciting journey taking you into a profession that is both academically stimulating and socially engaging. Medicine is about caring for the sick patient whether through the technical performance of a hip replacement by a large surgical team of surgeons, nurses and technicians or through the individual personal skills of a doctor engaged in the palliative care of a dying patient. Put another way, as it often is, Medicine is both an "Art and a Science" and you have to be a practitioner of both to be fully acknowledged by your patients as a "Doctor".

You will have had to achieve substantial academic success to reach this far but also you will have demonstrated personal qualities through interests in music, literature, theatre, film, art and many other disciplines, that we call the medical humanities, in order to achieve selection to your medical school. These personal pursuits, which you might consider as just extra curricular activities or a means of coping with stress, are an integral part of the hidden medical curriculum and key to your development as an humane doctor who can understand and take an interest in the individual patient and their everyday concerns.

This anthology of medical poetry has been created by two Consultant Physicians who have been involved in medical student education at Keele University for many years. Uniquely they are international award winning and published poets who are committed to medical humanities education. It is likely that you are not used to reading poetry or indeed consider that poems have little place in your struggle to master the metabolism of uric acid or the anatomy of the upper limb.

Medical poems however tell you what patients and doctors feel during the course of illnesses and treating illnesses. This is something you can't learn in lectures or out patient clinics. This little book of poetry acts as a vanguard for the medical humanities and our encouragement to you to continue all your interests in music, literature, theatre, film, the visual arts, and so many others, as a vital part of your medical education.
Treat the book with care and dip in from time to time.

Bruce Summers MB BS, FRCS, BA (Hons), MA (MedEd)
Consultant Orthopaedic and Spinal Surgeon
Senior Lecturer and Lead Tutor for Medical Humanities.
The University of Keele Medical School.

"Declare the past, diagnose the present, foretell the future."

Hippocrates

London Published as the Act directs December 31st 1815 by John Thomas Smith
No. 4 Chandos Street Covent Garden.

About Being A Doctor

Professor: This subject in addition to having his jugular vein severed was shot twice through the heart, in consequence of which he died. Now what would you do in a case like this?
Student: I would die too!

Advice to a Medical Student

Michael Swan

Well, good luck.
There is no finer career.

It won't be easy.

You will grow impatient
with some of your patients
for excellent reasons,
and make bad puns
to share with your colleagues.

Sometimes
you will save lives
but get no thanks.

Patients will die,
not your fault
but you will blame yourself.

A doctor friend of mine
said there are people
who will never forgive him
for what he knows about them.

Don't look for balance.
You can't cross the gulf
between our experience and yours.
Nor should you need to.

In a day's work
you may add immeasurably
to someone's quality of life,
and go home
to a quiet evening with your family.

Or you may give news
that will change lives
for the worse, for ever,
before a weekend's sailing.

Do the good that you can do
No one can do more.

Give what you can,
but
do not exceed the stated dose.

I honour your choice.
I thank you.

Venipuncture

John Graham-Pole

In the callows of my intern year of
sixty-seven, I kept the company of
big leukemia men, often so unstickable
I shrank from them; stuck so often
without issue but blasphemy of
tears leaking from the both of us.

I pinioned once a nameless tributary vein,
harnessed thick of shoulder, elbow,
supinated wrist at outermost rotation,
forcing a twist to the neck cords as
blue line on ulnar pulp bulged,
skittered squeamish, coy around my darts

until the time the hematoma sprang
screaming its livid tracer on the passes
of ineptitude, pricked me to sacrilege:
he'll die anyway (they all did then),
the blasphemy of blame: God why this
tiny vessel in this gargantuan frame?

Junior Doctor Learning Log
After Liz Berry

Karen Schofield

I have aimed bevelled needles between L3 and 4
and marvelled as spinal fluid fell drop by drop.

I have pierced arteries and countless veins,
watched cannulas fill with blood and saline flow,

worried about serum potassiums way too high
and puzzled over arterial gases when the pH was low.

I have recognised ST elevation on many ECGs
and spotted the pattern of atrial fibrillation

and listened to a thousand breaths in and out,
my stethoscope a fixture round my white coat.

I have watched the sunrise over hospital morgues
as the morning cast a cool light over my good works.

I have broken bad news and shared tears of grief
when there's no more to say and no need to speak

and turned away from results that shock
and learned when it's time to let a failing heart stop.

The Apprentice Surgeon

Michael Salcman

"death is the mother of beauty"
        —Wallace Stevens

How awful for him to cut the flesh or watch
a deep cut made before carbolic acid,
before ether, before hope was more than a wretch
on the kerb of the roadside, lungs etched

with cavitation and fawn-colored phlegm.
He knew how death would cork his mouth, killing his speech,
its beauty and necessity. Keats was an apprentice then
to death, his own and all of life beyond its reach:

the nightingale song, the clay of ancient Greece,
and that season of reconciliation for which he longed.
Entombed in life he felt no peace,
despaired of fame and got some of it wrong

while setting some right: dreamed of autumnal skies
while standing at the bedside, attending to the horror at Guy's.

GRAVE OF KEATS

IN THE PROTESTANT CEMETERY OF ROME

Having completed an apprenticeship with a GP and training at Guy's, on 25 July 1816, Keats sat his exams in Apothecaries Hall at Blackfriars. He passed with credit and became a qualified apothecary. He worked as a full time assistant to a surgeon for a short while and from all accounts was a competent medical practitioner.

Today I do not want to be a doctor

Glenn Colquhoun

Today I do not want to be a doctor.

Nobody is getting any better.

Those who were well are sick again
and those who were sick are sicker.

The dying think they will live.
And the healthy think they are dying.

Someone has taken too many pills.
Someone has not taken enough.

A woman is losing her husband.
A husband is losing his wife.

The lame want to walk.
The blind want to drive.
The deaf are making too much noise.
The oppressed are not making enough.

The asthmatics are smoking.
The alcoholics are drinking.
The diabetics are eating chocolate.

The mad are beginning to make sense.

Everyone's cholesterol is high.

Disease will not listen to me

Even when I shake my fist.

Today I want to be a doctor

Glenn Colquhoun

Today I am happy to be a doctor.

Everyone seems to be getting better.

Those who were sick are not so sick
And those who were well are thriving.

The healthy are grateful to be alive.
And the dying are at peace with their dying.

No one has taken too many pills.
No one has taken too few.

A woman is returning to her husband.
A husband is returning to his wife.

The lame accept chairs.
The blind ask for dogs.
The deaf are listening to music.
The depressed are tapping their feet.

The asthmatics have stopped smoking.
The alcoholics have stopped drinking.
The diabetics are eating apples.

The mad are beginning to make sense.

Nobody's cholesterol is high.

Disease has gone weak at the knees.

I expect him to make an appointment.

In All Those Years At Medical School

Roger Bloor

They never told me that sitting with the dying
was the human thing to do
I discovered that myself one night
behind the screens around a bed
at the end of the medical ward.

They never told me that all the family would want
was just for me to go upstairs and close her eyes
and place a bible in her hand
I discovered that myself one night
in the bedroom of that terraced house.

They never told me that fifty years later
I would still remember the name of the patient
who died before we could stop his bleeding
I discovered that myself last night
awaking from a dream-filled restless sleep.

They never told me how easily I would shed that tear
when a patient crossed the street to shake my hand
and wish me well for my retirement
I discovered that myself today
and thought that was a human thing for him to do.

it's about a man

Wendy French

it's about a man who healed the sick
as far as he was able
and this is the man who begged for penicillin
to cure a child
as far as he was able
it's about a man who burnt Fleming's letter
when the answer came back, None to Spare
and it's about a man who spoke at the funeral
as far as he was able
and this is the man who seven decades later
still remembers the date on the letter he wrote
it's about a man who waits in his chair
for a nurse to bring him whisky and water
this is the man who drinks the New Year in
although it's a man who can no longer hear
who peers out of his frame
as far as he is able
who thinks his own thoughts
it's about a man who comforted others
death is inevitable, comes to us all
it's about a man who is showered daily
and who now understands
as far as he is able

How to Behave with the Ill

Julia Darling

Approach us assertively, try not to
cringe or sidle, it makes us fearful.
Rather walk straight up and smile.
Do not touch us unless invited,
particularly don't squeeze upper arms,
or try to hold our hands. Keep your head erect.
Don't bend down, or lower your voice.
Speak evenly. Don't say
'*How are you?*' in an underlined voice.
Don't say, *I heard that you were very ill.*
This makes the poorly paranoid.
Be direct, say 'How's your cancer?'
Try not to say how well we look,
compared to when we met in Safeway's.
Please don't cry, or get emotional,
and say how dreadful it all is.
Also (and this is hard I know)
try not to ignore the ill, or to scurry
past, muttering about a bus, the bank.
Remember that this day might be your last
and that it is a miracle that any of us
stands up, breathes, behaves at all.

"Cure sometimes, treat often and comfort always."

Hippocrates

About Disease

Four Years After Diagnosis

Angela Narciso Torres

Suddenly, rain. Our heads
  bowed together like monks
in this hot green place.

  I study the slow script
of her movements. The cross
  and uncross of her legs,

fingers forking together,
  pulling apart. Secret dialect
of her face—a firefly flick

  in the iris, lips curling
like kelp. Speak, mother.
  Your daughter is listening.

A Seagull Murmur

Robin Robertson

is what they called it,
shaking their heads
like trawlermen;

the mewling sound of a leaking heart
        the sound
of a gull trapped in his chest.

To let it out
they ran a cut down his belly
like a fish, his open ribs

the ribs of a boat;
        and they closed him,
 wired him shut.

Caulked and sea-worthy now
with his new valve; its metal
tapping away:

the dull clink
        of a signal-buoy
or a beak at the bars of a cage.

Migraine

Fiona Sampson

A great unease...
as if you caused the storm
as if your body
were you its strange
clay its dirt-pressure filling
up the head

where the brain's tender tatters
cleave to themselves
poor brain and eyes poor cranium

Somewhere in a forest tender
shadows pass
between the leaves that turn
as they turn marvellous
and indescribable
all these birds and small creatures

Myeloma Moths

Karen Schofield

The moths came with a soft flutter
one night and burrowed into
the deepest recesses of cloth.

Their offspring had their fill, gnawed
the wool and cashmere mix of a coat
framed by a hanger, shaped like you.

They punched out holes, some like stars
which didn't shine, coalesced into craters.
Silver dust littered the wardrobe carpet.

They were driven out, killed off a few times,
but younger generations grew,
attacked the arms, shoulders and back

until the coat was held together by threads.
Shrunken and spineless its days were numbered,
it shed bits of blue wool like tears.

Mammogram

Jo McDougall

"They're benign," the radiologist says,
pointing to specks on the x-ray
that look like dust motes
stopped cold in their dance.
His words take my spine like flame.
I suddenly love
the radiologist, the nurse, my paper gown,
the vapid print on the dressing room wall.
I pull on my radiant clothes.
I step out into the Hanging Gardens, the Taj Mahal,
the Niagara Falls of the parking lot.

Coma

Mimi Khalvati

Mr Khalvati? Larger than life he was;
too large to die so they wired him up on a bed.
Small as a soul he is on the mountain ledge.

Lids gone thin as a babe's. If it's mist he sees
it's no mist he knows by name. Can you hear me,
Mr Khalvati? Larger than life he was

and the death he dies large as the hands that once
drowned mine and the salt of his laugh in the wave.
Small as a soul he is on the mountain ledge.

Can you squeeze my hand? (Ach! Where are the hands
I held in mine to pull me back to the baize?)
Mr Khalvati? Larger than life he was

with these outstretched hands that squeezing squeeze
thin air. Wired he is, tired he is and there,
small as a soul he is on the mountain ledge.

No nudging him out of the nest. No one to help him
fall or fly, there's no coming back to the baize.
Mr Khalvati? Larger than life he was.
Small as a soul he is on the mountain ledge.

The Memory Clinic

Roger Bloor

Set apart and distanced
by a woolly hat in a warm room,
passive and perplexed he waits
with 'why and when'
nipping at his worried heel.
Then Doreen, hand placed gently on his knee
calm and caring from her bag produces
flask and sandwiches
and in that brief distracted rest
from 'why and when' the two hold hands
and picnic in the past.

Chemo Nurse

Keith Chandler

How wonderful you are, bursting late
into this waiting room of politeness and fear
with its Hello/Country Life fantazines,
discreet fliers ('How to Stay Positive'),
help groups, homeopathic diets
and Chapel "just along the corridor"

without apology showing everyone
with a 'TA-DA!' whisk of your ocelot
the ladder running up your inside thigh
announcing without tact or holdback
in a half Brummie half Jamaican accent
how lucky it was you wore knickers today,

taking by the hand one by one
the women in not quite convincing wigs
or bald as an egg or surreal woollen hats
towards what you call your 'milking parlour',
talking 19 to the dozen so they hardly notice
being rigged up to the poison drips,

talking 19 to the dozen about the daughter
you left (late again) at her first school,
managing even among the moon-faced
and eyebrowless to raise a smile,
fitting the needle so they hardly notice
how difficult it is now to find a vein.

In this palace of fake cheerfulness
with its wipe clean smiles and flower prints
and a chaplain who asks if there is anything
all morning I hear naughty laughter
billowing out from behind the screens
and think: yes, you are The Real Thing.

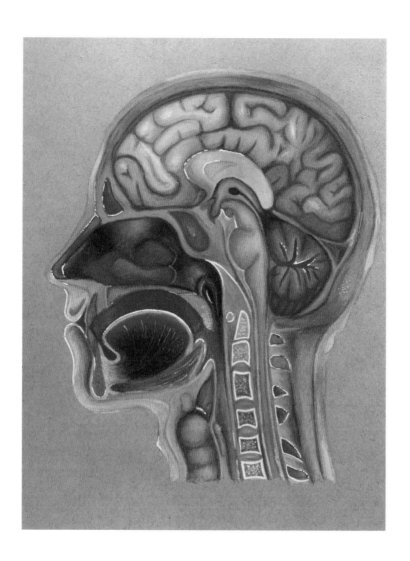

"The physician should not treat the disease but the patient who is suffering from it"
Moses Maimonides

About Being A Patient

In Intensive Care

Olivia Byard

It seems important to behave. Outbursts
only give hostage to the slavering beast
beyond the door. When nothing else
will work and the small body on the bed
struggles with each smaller breath, at least
there are manners; their elaborate rules.
So we play, near despair, a game of courtesy,
death on the advantage point.
Requests are made with extra care, complaints
swallowed whole: we hope somewhere
a kindly eye will notice that we tried
and order swift release. We do justice also
to our child's huge struggle,
keep it unmarred by the blots of every day,
and then we can say at whichever end,
we didn't let him down. So we smile
like professionals at the smiling staff
and carry on, knowing that if we stop
he will surely die and we shall be to blame.
Here, the balance is swung by feathers.

Too Heavy

Julia Darling

Dear Doctor,
I am writing to complain about these words
you have given me, that I carry in my bag
lymphatic, nodal, progressive, metastatic

They must be made of lead. I haul them everywhere.
I've cricked my neck, I'm bent
with the weight of them
palliative, metabolic, recurrent.

And when I get them out and put them on the table
they tick like bombs and overpower my own
sweet tasting words
orange, bus, coffee, June

I've been leaving them
crumpled up in pedal bins
where they fester and complain.
diamorphine, biopsy, inflammatory

And then you say
Where are your words Mrs Patient?
What have you done with your words?

Or worse, you give me that dewy look
Poor Mrs Patient has lost all her words, but shush,
don't upset her. I've got spares in the files.
Thank god for files.

So I was wondering,
Dear Doctor, if I could have
a locker,
my own locker
with a key.
I could collect them
one at a time,
and lay them on a plate
morphine-based, diagnostically,

with a garnish of
lollypop, monkey, lip.

Plane tree outside Ward 78

Helen Dunmore

The tree outside the window
Is lost and gone,
Billow of leaf in the summer dark,
A buffet of rain.

I might owe this tree to morphine,
1 might wake in the morning
To find it dissolved, paper
Hung in water,

Nothing to do with dreams.
I cannot sleep.
Pain is yards away
Held off like bad weather,

In the ward's beautiful contentment
Freed by opiates.
Hooked to oxygen
We live for the moment.

Leaving the Hospital

Anya Silver

As the doors glide shut behind me,
the world flares back into being –
I exist again, recover myself,
sunlght undimmed by dark panes,
the heat on my arms the earth's breath.
The wind tongues me to my feet
like a doe licking her newborn fawn.
At my back, days measured by vital signs,
my mouth opened and arm extended,
the nighttime cries of a man withered
child-size by cancer, and the bells
of emptied IVs tolling through hallways.
Before me, life – mysterious, ordinary –
holding off pain with its muscular wings.
Stepping to the curb, an orange moth
dives into the basket of roses
that lately stood on my sick room table,
and the petals yield to its persistent
nudge, opening manifold and golden

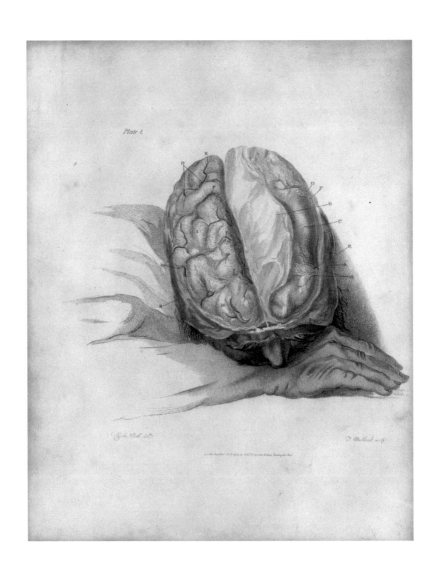

Plate 1.

44

The Poets

Angela Narciso Torres 27
Anya Silver 43
Fiona Sampson 29
Glenn Colquhoun 18, 19
Helen Dunmore 42
Jo McDougall 31
John Graham-Pole 14
Julia Darling 22, 40
Karen Schofield 15, 30
Keith Chandler 34
Michael Salcman 16
Michael Swan 12
Mimi Khalvati 32
Olivia Byard 39
Robin Robertson 28
Roger Bloor 20, 33
Wendy French 22

Notes on the Poets

Roger Bloor has published in several poetry magazines and anthologies including Magma and The Hippocrates Prize Anthology 2017 and 2019. His collection of Poems 'A Less Clear Dream' was shortlisted for the Arnold Bennet Book Prize 2018, and his poetry pamphlet 'Aldgedeslegh' was shortlisted in 2019. He was the winner of the Poetry London Clore Prize 2019. www.rogerbloor.co.uk

Olivia Byard is a British poet who grew up and attended university in Canada. Her third book of poetry, 'The Wilding Eye, New and Selected Poems', was published by The Worple Press in April, 2015, and became The New Statesman's recommended read. She is currently working on her fourth collection 'Crossing the Gulf'.

Keith Chandler is a retired school teacher, his poetry has been published in five collections by Carcanet, OUP, Redbeck, Peterloo, and Fairacre Press. His latest collection, The Goldsmith's Apprentice, published by Fair Acre Press in 2018, is the winner of the Rubery International Award for Poetry: Website: KeithChandlerPoet.com .

Glenn Colquhoun is a poet writer and doctor from New Zealand, 'Playing God' his third collection of poetry, detailed some of his experiences in medicine. It won the Reader's Choice prize at the Montana Books Awards. In 2006 it was awarded a Booksellers NZ Platinum Award for poetry. To date it has recorded sales of over 10,000 copies.

Julia Darling *(1956 – 2005)*, Julia's work encompassed a wide range of topics and forms from plays and novels to poetry and performance. She was an exceptional artist with a unique and humorous voice that engaged readers even when her work explored her declining health and ultimate death from cancer.

Helen Dunmore *(1952 - 2017)* was the author of 12 novels, including Orange Prize winner *'A Spell of Winter'*, as well as 10 poetry collections. Her poetry was recognised in a TS Eliot prize nomination, the Cardiff international poetry prize, the Alice Hunt Bartlett award and a win at the National Poetry Competition in 2010.

Wendy French has four full collections of poetry published and won the Hippocrates Poetry and Medicine prize for the NHS section in 2010 and was awarded second prize in 2011. She facilitates creative writing in healthcare settings. With Jane Kirwan she wrote the book *'Born in the NHS'*. She was Poet-in-Residence at the University College Hospital Macmillan Cancer Centre in 2015. *'Thinks Itself A Hawk'* is a product of that residency.

John Graham-Pole graduated from St Bartholomew's Hospital Medical School, he is emeritus professor of pediatrics, oncology, and palliative care from the University of Florida and specialised in caring for young patients with cancer. He has edited six books for non-professional readers—three non-fiction, three poetry—one of which won the William Carlos Williams Award.

Jacqualyn Walsh-House is currently a fourth year medical student at Keele University. Art has always been an important focus in her life since early childhood. Creating artwork provided her with opportunities to escape and process the more difficult life experiences.

Mimi Khalvati has published eight collections with Carcanet Press, including *'The Meanest Flower'*, shortlisted for the T S Eliot Prize, and *'Child: New and selected Poems'* a PBS Special Commendation. A new collection is forcoming in 2019. She is a fellow of the Royal Society of Literature.

Jo McDougall is a poet of the Arkansas Delta. Her work is noted for its sparseness and evocation of small-town life. Her poems are subtle portraits of the lives of rural families, farmers, housewives, and the struggles and tragedies they face. She has won many prizes for her work, in 2018, she was named Poet Laureate of Arkansas.

Abbie Randall is a fourth year medical student at Keele. Her love for the human form led her to draw a human eye when she was 12. Fascinated with drawing portraits and realism recently she has been pushing these ideas to the limits using bold colours and more surrealistic ideals.

Robin Robertson has published six books of poetry and received a number of accolades, including the E.M. Forster Award from the American Academy of Arts and Letters and all three Forward Prizes. '*The Long Take*', his book-length narrative poem, won the 2018 Roehampton Poetry Prize and the Goldsmiths Prize for Fiction, and was the first poem to be shortlisted for the Booker Prize.

Michael Salcman is an internationally known neurological surgeon, poet and art critic. Born in Pilsen, Czechoslovakia in 1946, the son of Holocaust survivors, he came to the United States in 1949 and started writing poetry while a student. His poetry collections include '*The Clock Made of Confetti*' (Orchises Press, 2007), nominated for The Poet's Prize in 2009, '*The Enemy of Good Is Better*' (Orchises, 2011), and '*A Prague Spring, Before & After*' (Evening Street Press, 2016).

Fiona Sampson was the Editor of *Poetry Review* from 2005-2012; she is now Editor of *Poem* and Professor of Poetry at the University of Roehampton, she has received, a number of Writer's Awards and various Poetry Book Society commendations. She has been shortlisted twice for both the T.S. Eliot Prize and the Forward Prizes. www.fionasampson.co.uk/.

Karen Schofield was awarded 3rd prize in the Hippocrates International poetry competition in 2016 and has had several commended poems published by the Hippocrates Press, 2015-2019. Her poem '*Myeloma Moths*' was published in '*Tools of the Trade, Poems for New Doctors',* by the Scottish Poetry Library, 2019.

Anya Silver published four poetry collections, *Second Bloom: Poems* (Cascade Press, 2017), *From Nothing: Poems*(Louisiana State University Press, 2016), *I Watched You Disappear* (Louisiana State University Press, 2014), and *The Ninety-Third Name of God* (Lousiana State University Press, 2010). She was named a Guggenheim Fellow in Poetry in 2018. She died of breast cancer in Georgia on August 6, 2018.

Pamela Sturges is currently a third-year medical student at Keele University. Throughout her life art and photography have been a constant. It is the difficult times in life that shape her artwork, using emotion and feelings to produce work with meaning or as a release.

Michael Swan is a widely published poet, his poems have been published in several poetry magazines and he has two published collections of poetry. He won The Poetry Society's 2010 Stanza Poetry Competition and third prize in the Hippocrates Poetry Competition 2019 *with 'Advice to a Medical Student'*.

Angela Narciso Torres is the author of *Blood Orange*, winner of the Willow Books Literature Award for Poetry. Recent work appears or is forthcoming in *POETRY, Missouri Review, Quarterly West, Cortland Review,* and *PANK.* She received First Prize in the 2019 Yeats Poetry Prize (W.B. Yeats Society of New York). *New City* magazine named her one of Chicago's Lit 50 in 2016. She serves on the editorial panel of *New England Review* and is a senior and reviews editor for *RHINO* Poetry.

Sources of Illustrations

Figure 1 Medicine Man - eye defect teaching models.
Wellcome Collection. CC BY i

Figure 2 A bearded man walking the streets with his hat
under his arm deeply engrossed in reading a book.
Etching by J.T. Smith, 1815. Credit: Wellcome
Collection. CC BY 9

Figure 3 A professor asking a medical student his prognosis
for a particular case. Coloured process print, 1900.
Wellcome Collection. CC BY 11

Figure 4 What We See - Jacqualyn Walsh-House 23

Figure 5 More Love - Abbie Randell 26

Figure 6 Head Over Heels - Abbie Randell 35

Figure 7 Patients waiting to see the doctor, with figures
representing their fears. Oil painting by Rosemary
Carson, 1997.Wellcome Collection. CC BY 38

Figure 8 Sir Charles Bell, The anatomy of the brain, 1802.
Credit: Wellcome Collection. CC BY 44

Keith Chandler: 'Chemo Nurse' reproduced by kind permission of the author, most recently published in *'Poems for the NHS'* (Onslaught Press 2018)

Olivia Byard: 'Intensive Care' reproduced by kind permission of the author. Published in, *'Strange Horses'*, Flambard Press, 2011.

Roger Bloor: 'The Memory Clinic' published in the *'Hippocrates Prize Anthology (2017)'*, 'In All Those Years at Medical School' published in the *'Hippocrates Prize Anthology (2019)'*.

www.clayhangerpress.co.uk

Printed in Great Britain
by Amazon